Beth Terry

Walking

in a

Crowd of Angels

A collection
by
Beth Terry

Published by:
Lezard Press, a division of Pacific Rim Seminars
P.O. Box 22664, Honolulu, Hawaii 96823, USA
Tel: 808.672.5008 • Fax: 808.672.5287
e-mail: Beth@BethTerry.com
web: http://www.BethTerry.com

Book and cover design: Joanmarie Ryan, Plum Productions
Cover image photographer: Bruce Heinmann

Library of Congress Cataloging-in-Publication Data
Terry, Beth
Walking in a Crowd of Angels: a collection by Beth Terry
p.   cm
ISBN: 0-9674769-0-9
1. Body, mind and spirit   2. Self-help
3. Family and Relationships   4. Philosophy   I. Title
LCCN: 99-091250

First Edition
10 9 8 7 6 5 4 3 2

This book is dedicated to my late father,
Condon H. Terry,
who believed in me
more than I believed in myself.

And to my husband Andrew,
who has shown me the true meaning
of unconditional love.

Acknowledgments

Special thanks to Joan Ryan *(of Plum Productions in Hawai'i),* for making sure this book actually made it into print. Thanks also to Stephanie Kendrick, for editing truthfully and with total understanding of who I am. To Tammy Shaw, for creative feedback. To my wonderful husband Andrew, for his steadfast love and belief in me. To my girls: Chenty, Liandra, Chaude and Alisha, for their contributions. To my sisters in the Imua Chapter of the American Business Women's Association for their great support. To Ted Sturdivant for his contacts and support. And, to my eight pound Chihuahua and muse, Lezard, for sitting on my lap during most of this writing, for keeping me amused and especially for keeping my heart open always to love.

Introduction

Through the many years I have presented motivational programs and training sessions, I have collected powerful and insightful observations on life. These have inspired me to put my own thoughts in writing. I share these with you: a collection of inspirational thoughts and ideas to make you pause and give you hope.

I have done my best to verify and gain permission to use those sayings that are not mine. Shakespeare, Voltaire and Goethe did not return my phone calls. Those who did, I thank you.

If you see a quote you feel is mis-attributed, or you know the author of an "unknown," I would appreciate hearing from you. If you have a quote you would like to see included in further editions, please send it along.

Enjoy!

To my friends: I need your help. Many people have been copying stories they love out of books and sending them to friends on the Internet. The problem is that the author and source disappear after a few forwards. Not only is this copyright infringement, it dilutes the power of the work and causes grievous pain to the soul of the author. Please enjoy the fruits of eight years labor and guard it well.

Contents

Perspective

The Angel

I sat on the library lawn of my college campus, contemplating ways to leave the planet. My roommate (I'll call her Mary) had systematically spent the previous year alienating every friend, male and female, that I had. Her manipulations at that time were completely unknown to me. All I knew was the un-returned phone calls, the first-dates with no call-backs, the looks of disdain on previously friendly faces.

Convinced that I was of no use to anyone; certain that I was more in the way than of any help, I decided I would quietly take care of all obligations and slip off the planet without anyone noticing or caring.

I was so engrossed in my plans that I didn't notice her walk up. Suddenly a beautiful Chinese woman was in my face, her long black hair startling me out of my reverie. "You are 'Mary's' roommate, right?" I nodded. "Good, I caught you before you did something stupid." Scowling, I told her to go away. She persisted, "Look, I was Mary's roommate and I have to talk with you. You seem like a nice girl. She's not. You need to know that."

Now she had my attention. "Last year I was sitting where you are, contemplating an honorable way to commit suicide without shaming my family. I know that is what you are doing. It's not you, it's her."

I started to cry and she wrapped her arm around my shoulder while she detailed the manipulations and warped behavior of a roommate who wanted to own the souls of those she lived with. Mary had faked several diseases and had "broken" a wrist to get sympathy. She had lied to, stalked and threatened others who had gotten close to me in the past year. I was in a movie; this couldn't be real.

A tremendous weight lifted as this mysterious woman made sense of my life over the past twelve months. She told me to go and check her story with trusted friends who were "pre-Mary." Then she hugged me and disappeared.

I checked first with an old boyfriend. Sure enough, Mary had paid him a disturbing visit. She had spun a web of stories about my supposed trickery and pathology and had made him decide to stay away. Her line was always, "Well, you know, I *am* Beth's best friend, and I know everything there is to know about her. I can't believe she is doing this, but I'm trying so hard to help her." When I asked him why he didn't first check with me, he said, "Well, I didn't want to get caught in a meat grinder."

Stunned, I kept going. One classmate after another confirmed the stories. Within 24 hours I had enough evidence to do something. I went home, packed all my belongings, and began to move into a new place. When Mary came home, I told her she was a sick puppy and needed to get help. That was all. No need to get hysterical or accusatory. I knew I was right, and I knew this was the only way to save my soul.

I looked for the Asian woman. I thought she had said her name was Heidi Chang. I looked in the school directory. No such name. I asked Mary's old friends. None had remembered an Asian woman as her roommate. I looked in the yearbook. No picture of this woman. I checked several campuses in the area. No one fit her description.

I only thought of her again one year later. I was getting ready to go riding on a motorcycle with a boyfriend. Just before he arrived, I heard a voice in my head. It sounded vaguely familiar, it was Heidi's voice. She said, "You can't go with him. Don't go." As he pulled up, I felt wind in my face and a definite tugging at my shoulder. Then the voice again, "Don't go." When he came to the door, I made excuses and promised to see him later that weekend. He went to the dirtbike course without me. His bike crashed in a ravine and he spent the next several weeks in the hospital.

If I had been on that bike...?

Who is Heidi? I don't know. I'm alive thanks to her. She has been one of the myriad of Angels who travel in my world. Spirit or mortal, beings like her have carried me through some of the toughest times of my life. They show up when I need them. They give me the information and hope to carry on.

I'm convinced that I am walking this world in a crowd of angels.

Beth Terry

"A hen is only an egg's way of making
another egg."

Samuel Butler (1835-1902)

"I love avocados.
When avocado season rolled around,
I was the first one at the store, poring over the
green silken fruit.
Then I got an avocado tree.
Now I don't eat them anymore.
Abundance creates indifference."

Beth Terry

"If there were no flagrantly bad people around, the consciously virtuous would be deprived of much of their pleasure."

Author Unknown

"If fifty million people say a foolish thing,
it is still foolish."

Anatole France (1844-1924)

"There is no such thing as certainty.
All that we are certain of is the recent past.
And with age, even that is suspect."

Beth Terry

"The awareness of the ambiguity
of one's highest achievements
(as well as one's deepest failures)
is a definite symptom of maturity."

Paul Tillich (1894-1965)

Do I Know You?

I read today that squirrels are hit by cars because they are not calibrated to see anything moving at sixty miles per hour. Humans can't hear dog whistles because our ears aren't calibrated for that pitch. It's as though we are all given different windows from which to view the world: some of us have mountain views and some of us have ocean views. (And some people got the view of the parking garage...)

I only know you through the window of my experience. If I am one-dimensional, I will see you as one-dimensional, and you may have qualities that I cannot understand through my narrow window. When I expand myself, I expand my ability to see you, because my window is wider and I may be able to finally find you around a previously unknown corner. I owe it to myself and to you to expand myself.

When I do that, I give you the gift of understanding and compassion, and you will be encouraged to expand yourself, passing on the same gifts to others. Peace in the world comes one windowpane at a time.

Beth Terry

"We intercede on behalf of all mankind.
Then we do laundry."

A Thai monk (1991)
after being asked his mission in life

"Listen, darling, no one ever makes it past the age of twelve. When you get that, you'll be just fine..."

Worldly advice from
my grandmother, Florence Sholk
on my 16th birthday

"You know you're a grown-up when you have a cabinet full of candy and don't feel the need to eat all of it at one sitting."

Carol Terry

Pretty Soon

My first-grade stepdaughters struggled with their homework: learning to tell time. Fraternal twins, they have developed very different ways of learning, even at this early age. One of them is very literal. To her, life is black and white and there is little room for the abstract. The other is a dreamer, always using fanciful words and figurative expressions. I overheard them talking as they studied. My literal one wanted to know when the dreamer was going to finish her homework so they could move on to the next project. The dreamer kept saying, "Pretty soon, pretty soon." Finally in exasperation, the literal one stood up, pointed at the clock on the wall, and said,

"There *IS NO* 'Pretty Soon' on the clock!"

Beth Terry

"Of course he's a boy!
His mother's still alive,
so how could he grow up?"

*Chaude Bonifacio at 6 years old,
while determining whether Daddy
should get a Boys' Day present*

Once an ancient rural custom, then an elaborate festival for the well-being of boy children in Japan, Boys' Day (5/5) is now Children's Day, a national Japanese holiday. Hawai'i is the only place in the world that still celebrates the traditional Boys' Day.

Well... It *WAS* Motivational

As owner of a seminar company, I am always looking for good stories to make my point. I was happy that I had finally found the famous time-line for Abraham Lincoln, and I flashed it on the overhead projector during my "What a Difference You Can Make!" seminar. I was proving that we *all* can succeed if we only persevere.

I read off the dates to the class: "1831: failed in business; 1832: ran for legislature and was defeated; same year, failed in business again and had a nervous breakdown; 1838: ran for speaker and was defeated; 1840 ran for elector and was defeated; on and on through the political races of 1843, 1848, 1855, 1856 and 1858, all in which Abraham Lincoln was defeated." I triumphantly then pronounced: "And yet, in 1860, Abraham Lincoln *finally* reached success. He was elected President of the United States of America!"

And a tired, cynical voice piped up in the back row. . . "and then they shot him."

Beth Terry

"I suppose that God gave us all those books
and bibles and writings to keep us busy.
S/He must be sitting up there chuckling
at all our self-important dialogues,
diatribes and dissertations.
If you know the Truth,
all our opinions
must be mighty amusing."

Beth Terry

What if...

What if on December 31 at midnight, there is a great clap of thunder, and a deep belly laugh heard 'round the world. What if God, lets out an exuberant guffaw and whispers in our heads in each of our own languages, "OK, kids! That's a wrap. What did you learn?"

What if this *IS* really a test.

What if each person who has irritated you, angered you, challenged you, made you feel less than yourself, or made you feel inferior... what if those persons were here on assignment... and they were assigned to *YOU?* What if their mission has been to help you grow and come home to yourself? What if your only purpose here is to cultivate your soul... to hone your ethical, sacred Being... to become connected at the core to the "Universal One Who Loves Us" even in our imperfection?

What if at the end of this, the "Universal One Who Loves Us" still loves us, no matter how we did on the test?

What if the question is not "How many sins did you commit?," but, "Did you learn from every mistake, every sin? And what was it that you learned?"

What if the "perfect" ones, the ones who never own up to mistakes, the ones who never learn because they never admit wrongdoing, what if *they* are the ones who flunked this class?

Think about how much you know, and why you know it. My child does not remember the problems she got *right* on the practice test. She remembers the problems she got wrong: the ones she and I wrestled with to find the answers. On the final exams, she aces the difficult problems. The easy problems are an ancient memory, and answers don't come so easily.

We are who we are because of the problems that frustrate us and tangle us into knots. Each step towards resolution adds a layer of texture to our character and toughness to our skin. We can handle more at fifty than we could at twenty. We know more, we bounce back better. We let the small stuff slide… or, at least we are supposed to.

What did you learn? Could you answer that if it were your day in court? I will give it a try:

"Well, Divine Creator, what did I learn? I learned that it is better to cooperate with people than to fight. I learned that if you forgive, the hurting goes away faster. I learned that revenge and vindictiveness hurt me more than they do my target. I learned that I am not perfect and it is OK with me because it's OK with you. I learned that love sometimes does hurt, and it's worth it anyway. I learned that sometimes love comes in the form of a lecture or a swift kick in the seat of my pants, and if I just listen, I'm usually better off."

"I learned that not everyone is entitled to my opinion. I learned what it is to try and make a silk purse of a sows ear. And I don't cast pearls before swine."

"I learned that children are here to remind us that life must go on, and that bursting into spontaneous exuberance is still a viable option, even at my age. I learned that nothing, but nothing, heals depression like a good belly laugh and a child's stubby little arms wrapped around my neck. I learned that skipping and running are good for the soul. I've learned that the gift of children is their eyesight. They magically see through the most self-righteous and impenetrable of masks."

"I learned that my worries dissolve like a teaspoon of sugar in the ocean when I simply give them over to you. I learned that trusting you is probably the best idea I've ever had, and I'm never sorry when I listen to you and take your advice."

"And mostly, I've learned that I do have a gift, and that you have a plan for that gift, and all I need to do is breathe deeply and follow it. The fact that I have a gift does not make me better than anyone. It is *my* gift. Everyone has one. We all need to stop resisting our gifts and just use them the way You intended.

If we don't, our lives will be crowded with those teachers trying to bring us back home to ourselves."

What if . . .

What if life is a seminar exercise?

What if the "Great Judgment Day" is just a debriefing?

What did you learn?

How will you use it to improve?

How's your soul doing after the lesson?

Beth Terry

"**G**et over yourself **!**"

God,
your mother,
your siblings,
your employer,
and many, many others

Just think about this...

In 80 years, everything from the size of your thighs to the size of your bank account won't matter to anybody. All the stuff you're working so hard to accumulate has one of three fates:

- Your heirs will fight over it and ruin their family ties; or

- It will be packed up and set on the curb for the Salvation Army; or

- The trash truck will haul it away.

So take a deep breath and enjoy who you are, where you are, and how you are —right now, right here.

Beth Terry

Moving Beyond
Self-Imposed Limits

"Whatever you can do
or dream you can,
begin it.
Boldness has genius, power
and magic in it."

Johann Wolfgang Von Goethe (1749-1832)

"We are what we repeatedly do.
Excellence then, is not an act, but a habit."

Aristotle (384-322 BC)

"Pray that success will not come any faster
than you are able to endure it."

Elbert Hubbard (1865-1915)

The Arrogance of Insecurity

Insecurity is its own form of arrogance. Or worse, it is heresy of the highest order: "And God created the heavens and the earth, and all that is within them..." (except, God, you did a lousy job with me...).

How dare we even *think* to be insecure about this wondrous creation? No computer, no robot, no contraption with miles of cables and millions of computer chips can *begin* to recreate this combination of mind, body and soul! It grows, it expands, it is self-healing, self-teaching, able to re-create itself, able to communicate with a variety of species, able to problem solve, and, most importantly, able to love. That alone is worthy of our highest respect.

How dare we give ourselves so much credit to think that we have a right to criticize this creation of God? And, more importantly, why? Yes, we should note when we are not being all that we were created to be, and that should make us ask, "So, what do I do now? What can I learn now? What is it that makes me do that, be that, want that? What is it I can do to contribute to humanity?"

Insecurity appears only in humans and the animals that hang around with us. We do not see insecure palm trees trying to grow papayas or a daisy wishing vainly to smell like a rose.

Don't give in to the temptation of insecurity. Don't use the weak excuse that you are not enough!!! Be your beautiful self. Be your imperfect, too-loud, too-quiet, too-everything self. In all your glory and magnificence you were created to be and do only one thing in this life —be yourself. In that self you will find meaning, love, service, support and expansion.

Time spent in self-flagellation not only diminishes your potential, it is painful for others in your life who have to spend time with you while you whine. Give us all a rest! Look in the mirror today and thank God for your existence. Get healthy. Get whole. Then get out there and do something useful!

Beth Terry

"A person's destiny is a private affair,
you can only provide whatever tools necessary
for them to make it in the world
in their own time."

Burl Burlingame
Honolulu Star Bulletin, 1984

"All privileges come with their own perils . . .
all perils come with their own privileges."

Beth Terry

"The important thing is this:
to be able at any moment
to sacrifice what we are for what
we could become."

Charles Du Bois

"Personal power is having
access to and control over your feelings
and ways of thinking in any situation."

Olaf Isaachson, 1987

"Self-improvement is not about
changing who you are;
it's about releasing the barriers and
becoming *FULLY* who you are."

Beth Terry

"Instead of being a victim and using revenge-type thinking, realize that revenge keeps you down and damages your soul. Revenge is a downward cycle and keeps you in the victim game.

Try focusing on solutions. When you use solution-based thinking, when you ask 'Now what?' you are on the road to recovery. You are on the road home to yourself."

Beth Terry

Focus on the Future

He is peaceful as he walks around the gym. If the team isn't working out, he exercises on the machines. Occasionally, he walks over to an aspiring weightlifter and mentions a few things that might help them lift better.

When I first saw this handsome man in his late fifties, he seemed knowledgeable and I appreciated his thoughtful suggestions, so it was logical to ask if he was a personal trainer, and was he looking for more clients. He just chuckled and said he didn't do this for pay.

From time to time, I'd see him and ask his advice about this lift or that weight machine. He always delivered clear instructions, thoughtfully and politely. One day he asked me if I would like to be on the Hawaii Olympic Weightlifting team. I accepted immediately. I began to notice how all the other lifters paid attention to this man. And one Saturday,

I found out why.

People were patting him on the back; shaking his hand; giving him the high sign. Someone brought in the clipping from that morning's paper. He had been inducted into the Olympic Hall of Fame. This was Tommy Kono! This man had overcome asthma as a small child; had lived in a WWII American concentration camp for Japanese; had won gold medals in the 1951 and 1956 Olympics, and had made a name for himself in war weary America and the world. A Japanese man who had overcome his own fears, his own physical problems, and the prejudice of a country still reeling from two Asian wars in as many decades.

He was my coach before I knew he was "somebody." And that's what makes him so special. He is a gentleman's gentleman. He radiates peace and confidence. He is a man who has made his mark and has nothing to prove. He spends his life giving himself away... he has made an incredible impact in the lives of thousands of young people.

I learned firsthand what made Tommy Kono a champion. Shortly after his induction, I told him I would be traveling on the mainland and would like a place to work out and prepare for my first competition. He gave me the name of a fellow Olympian who had a gym I could use.

As soon as my plane landed, I checked in at the hotel and hurried off to find my temporary coach. As I walked in, he hollered, "Are you from Kono's team?" I told him I was and he said, "Good. Start warming up." As I lifted the 45 pound bar, he barked, "What's the matter with you? Put some weights on that thing!" Cross-eyed and out of breath, I struggled to warm up with more than the usual weight. He barked again, "God, where did you get those shoes?" I wheezed, "Tommy told me to wear them." He rolled his eyes and said, "Oh well, show me what you can do."

Already a bit discouraged, I steeled myself and decided I would just make the best of this. I breathed, centered myself and prepared for my first lift, struggling to remember all I had been taught. As I started to pull, he shouted, "What is taking so long, c'mon, c'mon!" I lifted badly, and tried to get focused again.

All through the workout, he rolled his eyes, shook his head and yelled at me. An hour later, I walked out of the gym a defeated soul.

On the flight home to Honolulu, I composed a reasonable, rational speech for Tommy, explaining why I would not be competing or staying on his team. I walked into the gym on Saturday morning prepared to quit. Tommy saw me and asked why I was not dressed for the workout. I gave my speech about being too old for the team and taking too much of his time, and not being very good. After all, I was starting out at 38 and he was 35 when he retired from lifting. He chuckled and said softly, "Oh yeah, I forgot to tell you about him. Go get dressed."

For the next two hours, Tommy worked patiently with me. He watched me, then said, "That was good. Now, next time, focus on your arch." And then, "OK, better. Now, next time, remember your arms are like ropes and give me good arch." "Great. That was just great. Now, next time power through with your legs and lean a bit further over the bar." "OK, good. Next time, let's see you add a little bit more weight."

Next Time! Next Time! Next Time! All morning he focused my attention on the next thing. All morning I was facing in the direction of success, instead of looking back on a stupid mistake or failure on my part.

He told me later, "It is best not to exaggerate and bring mistakes to the forefront. Doing that makes the student think in the wrong direction. If you want to help them, have them think about the right way to do something." We've heard that well-known motivational mantra, "Where the attention goes, the energy flows." That proved true for me.

Because of Tommy's patient approach, I lifted 80 pounds over my head for the first time that day.

The week before, at the end of my discouraging workout, I could barely lift the 45 pound bar. Because of Tommy's instruction, over the next five years,
I won three gold medals and three first place trophies in local competition. One of those earned me a Hawai'i state record.

One more time, I am better because someone believed in me more than I did. This angel saw opportunity where I saw failure.

Beth Terry

Popsicles

The twins ran home excitedly one day from school. They had learned the hand motions to a popular song, "I Can See Clearly Now." As they performed the song, I had to struggle to keep from laughing. These optimistic youngsters had run into an "obstacle" and completely changed the meaning of the song. They belted out with all their little might,

"I can see clearly now the rain has gone.
I can see all POPSICLES in my way!"

Beth Terry

Mental & Emotional Health

"People who cannot find time for recreation
are obliged sooner or later
to find time for illness."

John Wanamaker, 1893

"Sweet are the uses of adversity."

Shakespeare (1564-1616)

"Each man lives in the prison of his own ideas."

Albert Einstein (1879-1955)

"What you are speaks so loud,
I can't hear what you say."

Voltaire (1694-1778)

"There are two ways of being happy:
we may either diminish our wants or augment our
means. Either will do, the result is the same.
And it is for each man to decide for himself and do
that which happens to be the easiest."

Benjamin Franklin (1706-1790)

"Risk Risk Risk!
You can't keep your foot on First
and steal second!"

Anonymous

"There is only one success —to be able to spend
your own life in your own way."

Christopher Morley (1890-1957)

"There is no cure for birth and death,
save to enjoy the interval."

George Santayana (1863-1952)

"May you live all the days of your life!"

Jonathan Swift in "Gulliver's Travels" (1667-1745)

You Make a Difference !!!

You have lived through much. You have much to share: both your pains and your triumphs. This is a world that needs to hear what you have to say. There will be time to rest later. *WE NEED YOU NOW!*

There's a thought in the Bible that is shared by many of the world's religions — You are Blessed so that you might **BE** a Blessing:

"And God said to Abram, go from your country, your kindred and your father's house to a land that I will show you. And I will make you a great nation; I will bless you *so that you will be a blessing.* I will bless those who bless you, and him who curses you, I will curse. And through you *all the families of the earth shall bless themselves."* Genesis 12: 1-3

There are many ways to share yourself with others so that you can be a blessing. Much of it is accomplished simply by being emotionally conscious. Today's children, today's young people, today's men and women in mid-life crises need the kind of support you can give. You've been through it... you can give to them by:

- encouraging them
- trusting them
- respecting them
- letting them glimpse your failures
- letting them share your successes
- showing them what quality and pride mean
- embracing them as viable members of the community
- expecting more from them than they do from themselves
- most importantly: reminding them of the lessons you learned so their path might be a little smoother.

Beth Terry

"When we permit these dark perceptions to dominate us, we are allowing our future to be shaped by visions that are small and mean and diminishing to our potential."

Author Unknown

"There are a lot of people out there
who are willing to say bad things
about you and to you.
You shouldn't be one of them."

Beth Terry

Three Things We All Want

After traveling around the world, and giving presentations to over 200,000 people in the past thirty years, I have noticed that we are all more alike than different. In fact, most of us have these three things in common with the rest of the humans living on the planet:

1. We just want to make it through our day!
2. We want to better our situation in life.
3. We want to take care of someone we love.

That pretty much sums it up. Keep that in mind the next time you run into someone you think is different from you.

Beth Terry

Four Things We All Need

Human beings are strange, weird, ornery creatures. We get under each others' skin, sometimes intentionally. We argue for the sake of arguing. We think that stubbornness is a virtue. When things are going well, we are suspicious that just around the corner lurks disaster, or we do something monumentally stupid to insure that we will sabotage that peace. And, we can also be pretty wonderful. If we look inside, we will realize that, like the three things we want, there are four things we all desire deep in our hearts. We don't just desire them —we expect them. And when we don't get these things, we get hurt, angry, or... even.

These four deep-seated needs are:

1. To Be Respected
2. To Be Appreciated
3. To Be Understood
4. To Feel Welcome

When those four things are present, we are happy. Giving these to others is the grease in the cogs of life, smoothing the way for cooperation and communication. When they are absent —*watch out!* This is also self-preservation! —"When people don't get respect, they get attorneys!"

Beth Terry

"Pain can expand you or contract you;
open you up or shut you down.
Choose.

Beth Terry

"Your life is defined by the choices you make
minute by minute, day by day.
We improve or sabotage ourselves
one breath at a time."

Beth Terry

Wonder

It was the end of a heavy training week: twelve seminars in five days, two on the Neighbor islands. Exhausted, I waited in the standby line to see if I could get out of Kona earlier. The last available seat was mine.

In the cabin, I squinted bleary eyes to find the last seat. It was in the middle of 34 second graders from Liholiho School and their *very tired* chaperones.

With every turn of the plane, wonder filled the air. Happy noises emanated from 34 little bodies. Wonder at the ocean, the lava, *free* soda, trays that go up *and* down, seats that move, lights and overhead air ducts. Spontaneous giggles with no apparent cause. Whirligig toys. Kinetic energy that evidently had the chaperones drained of all life. Most of them were asleep.

Where does the energy come from? And why do grown-ups lose it? Bills, family, job stress?

We lose wonder.

My goal for the rest of this year is to rediscover wonder. Burst into spontaneous exuberance. Who cares what other grown-ups think? Maybe this will be contagious.

I got off the plane and realized I wasn't tired anymore. Spontaneous exuberance... what a concept! What a great goal! I laughed all the way to the parking garage.

Beth Terry

Chaude Bonifacio

Lessons

Your Birth Date

Today's Date

Blessings and Lessons

• Write down your birthday •

• Write today's date •

• Draw a circle around it •

Look at that circle —it is your life; the sum total of who you are. In that circle are all your experiences: all the dumb things you did, all the hurtful things you have said. In there too, is all the pain inflicted on you by others.

You can't change it, not one moment of it, and you shouldn't. These events are what have given you character, texture and compassion. These experiences helped define you and teach you life's lessons.

In truth, there are only two things in that circle that matter: the lessons and the blessings. Lessons are learned in pain: "I won't do that again," or "I won't let anyone do that to anyone else." Those are powerful motivators. The blessings come to give you joy, if you are willing to recognize them.

No, you can't go back and change anything. But you can forgive and move on. You can let go and create anew.

All we have is ***TODAY***.

One *glorious*, delightful gift of a day.

How will you live today?
What will you do with your time?
How you spend each moment is how you spend your life.
Will you waste your time in sadness and despair?
Will you spend your time in negative attitudes,
        laziness, unproductive thoughts and actions?
Will you renew yourself: making and keeping promises,
        supporting others, using your talents?

What do you want from this life?
What do you want in your relationships?
What is your vision for your future? For the future of
        this earth and your time on it?

Choose it! Look at your life as a play that is being written. Take the pen in hand and write it for yourself. Make it happen!

Learn the lessons.
Celebrate the blessings!

See, there is another circle that is more important than the first. It is the circle that starts today and ends when you leave the planet. Fill it with hope, joy and fulfillment.

Get out there and be the blessing you were meant to be!

Beth Terry

Lessons on Life
from a Game of Solitaire

♠ No matter how good the hand looks,
sometimes you still can't win.

♥ If you keep trying to milk a hand, you may
find that you are just delaying being dealt the
winning hand.

♣ Winning a hand sometimes depends on only
one card — if you miss that card, you might
think you have a weak hand.

♦ If you stay in the game, sooner or later,
you will win.

♠ Even if you could go back and replay a hand,
it probably would still turn out the same.

♥ Some hands aren't winners,
even though they'll get you awfully close.

♣ Just because it is easy and flows in the beginning doesn't mean it's a winning hand — maybe you just blew all the good luck at the beginning.

♦ Trust your instincts — when it feels like a bad hand, let it go.

♠ Most of the time, if you follow the formula, you will win — sometimes the only way to win is to forget the formula.

♥ Winning means going one step beyond where everyone else goes.

♣ You are more awake when there is a lot of action in the cards; it is easy to miss an opportunity when you are hypnotized by a slow pace.

♦ Sometimes what looks like a bad hand can be turned around with just one card. If you quit too early, you'll never know...

Beth Terry

Christmas Every Day

There were eight of us kids, and in my 16th year, money was so tight that the only presents under the tree were bought with baby-sitting and paper-route money. Our wrapping paper was made in craft class.

In each stocking were carefully rolled parchments — notes from my father. My letter started with, "My Beautiful Daughter Beth. I am so proud of who you are and what you do. You have been blessed with so many gifts: I love the way you make us all laugh...," and he went on to list everything his 40-year old eyes saw in this gawky 16-year old kid.

He ended his long letter with, "Remember that you have been given these gifts not to hoard, but to share with a world that needs you. I expect great things from you and I believe in you. I love you, Your Daddy."

With nine letters full of hope, love and acknowledgments (my Mom got one, too), Dad reminded us what this season is all about. And he gave me the only Christmas gift I remember in all my years of "getting."

Today, when there's no parking at the mall, you can't find the right "toy du jour," and the cashier's line looks hopeless, think about a gift of love and praise instead. Put some hope in a Christmas stocking...

Let someone know you believe in them.

Beth Terry

Just because they ask you to dance...

One day my dad asked me why I was always fighting with my boyfriend. I told him I didn't care much for the guy anymore. He was always bossing me around and trying to control my life. Since I was sixteen and my boyfriend was almost twenty, this was probably a great relief for my dad to hear. "But," Dad asked, "If you don't like him, why are you still together?" I thought about it a while and said, "Because he asked me to go steady, and that's what I'm doing." Dad smiled and said, "Honey, just because they ask you to dance, doesn't mean you have to. Just because they say they like you, doesn't mean you have to like them back. Life doesn't always involve an even exchange. How they feel about you is their business. How you feel about yourself when you are with them, is *YOUR* business." I broke up with my boyfriend that afternoon.

Beth Terry

things. I learn.

1 I learn things BY doing.

2 I learn BY listening.

3 I learn BY making mistakes.

4 I learn BY trying again.

5 I learn BY watching.

6 I learn BY thinking.

7 I learn BY paying attention.

8 I learn BY useing my brain.

9 I learn BY useing my senses.

Alisha Bonifacio, age 8
First attempt at computer graphics project,
complete with her own spelling

"This doesn't look like Love,
but it is!!!"

*Mom Terry while sending young Beth
to her room for the umpteenth time*

Time Out

In a family meeting with the girls, my husband Andrew was discussing the virtues of discipline. At elementary school age, they are trying to grasp that being put on restriction is a good thing; that discipline is one of the life lessons that will make you healthy and sane later on in life. As they discussed it, and told him that their friends didn't get time outs, he sighed and said,

"Look, if you don't get enough time outs as a kid, you will get plenty of them as a grown up!"

Beth Terry

Thoughts on the Ten Commandments

I never see the ten commandments as orders from an angry god. These aren't impossible house rules from a puritanical, disciplinarian, vindictive Being... but rather Wisdom from a Loving Source.

In order to get the Ten Commandments, think like a child. The real message is simple and clear:

Don't do anything that makes your soul feel yucky.

Thou shalt honor your parents,
> because when you are one you will realize they did the best they knew how. They kept your little body clothed and warm, they fed you and provided shelter, they educated you, bought your fundraising tickets, put up with you and even laughed at your dumb jokes. And, the universe has a way of balancing out. How you treated your parents is how your kids will treat you!

Thou shalt not covet thy neighbor's stuff,

because it makes you forget how lucky you are to have as much as you already do. And if he has more than you, maybe he was willing to give up all those fast-food nights out and those impulse items so he could save enough to have what he has. Coveting also makes you want to do silly things, like take what is not yours. Which is part two of this commandment:

Thou shalt not steal,

because then thou doesn't recognize the value of that which was not earned or given freely. This causes grievous pain to the soul, and makes all your neighbors suspicious of you. Plus, it's just dumb, because, sooner or later you'll get caught.

Thou shalt not commit adultery,

because it poisons your own soul and makes you look for reasons to give up the love you already have. You then become uncomfortable in the presence of your beloved, and in your guilt, will eventually take it out on your new love. This is not about the law. This is about self-respect. Adultery usually ends in self-loathing and creates a numbness where compassion should live.

Thou shalt not kill.

Do I really have to explain this? I asked a little boy once why it was wrong to kill. He said, "Because if you do, then every night their ghost will stand at the end of your bed and you'll have to keep saying, 'Sorry!'" That about sums it up.

Thou shalt not bear false witness.

If you lie, you have to keep track of your stories. If you tell the truth, you only have to remember what happened. Makes life way easier. Plus, lying is dumb and makes people think you are running for office. Can't have that kind of rumor being spread about you!

Thou shalt not have false Gods or graven images.

Hey– just stay focused on what is important! Don't get carried away with stuff that won't support your soul or keep love in the world. Not that hard!

Thou shalt observe the Sabbath.

God didn't need a degree in psychology to tell us to take a break now and again. He's saying, "Relax and set yourself down and appreciate all that I have made for you. I love you, now take a deep breath!"

Thou shalt not take the name of the Lord in vain.

The name of the Lord is "I AM". When you say bad stuff about the "I AM", you are saying bad stuff about yourself. I heard once that we are all like shards of the mirror known as God. Even in the tiniest piece of mirror, we can see a complete reflection. Get that you are a piece of that Being known as God, "I AM". And stop being so hard on yourself.

Love the Lord your God with all your heart, mind and soul and your neighbor as yourself.

Well now, this is the summary statement for the whole treatise. If you are focused on Love, life's questions just clear up. What is the loving thing to do? How can I focus on love while I am solving today's challenge?

See, this is all about being gentle with and loving the sweet soul that resides in you. Even if you have not met that soul, it is there waiting for you to set aside those ideas and attitudes that damage the part of you that holds you together. Your soul has your highest good as its goal. Don't do anything that will harm it.

Beth Terry

"We are not here to make a living,
we are here to make a life."

Walter E. Russell
"The Man Who Tapped the Secrets of the Universe" c.1921

Change

"Change is inevitable, and it's damned uncomfortable. Yet, without it you would still be crawling around in your diapers. The best way to survive when change happens is to say,
'Oh Well!!'
Not, 'Oh well, I give up'... but
'Oh Well... Now What?'"

Beth Terry

LOVE is a Four Child Word

I had carefully constructed my life to indulge my free spirit. For years I lived in a beautiful little house atop the hills above Waikiki, traveled at my whim and enjoyed the good life. I was responsible only for myself. Then, I fell in love. Fell? Crashed, burned, collided is closer to the truth. I thought my new love was 35, he thought I was 33. He was 27, I was 41, and he came fully loaded: four children and relatives enough to fill a small plantation town. That was a container-load of baggage to add to my peaceful, monk-like existence.

I fought the soaring feelings at first. Many months went by before this magical man was allowed passage into my world. And more than a year more before we discovered that he was to have custody of his girls. With that revelation came the earthquake: he couldn't do this alone, could they all move in? My ego and free spirit fought mightily. My pastor's heart won. Into my home came four-year old twins, weeks shy of their fifth birthday. A demure six-year old and a sub-limely funny, feisty tomboy of nine.

I gamely held on to my sanity, as I wrestled with the implications of step-motherhood. This was not how I'd visualized flowing into my fabulous forties. The summer trudged by, trampling my solitude, ripping away all hope for meditation and quiet thought. The surprises were wonderful, frightening, comical. Children have a way of sneaking into your heart when you are looking elsewhere. And their logic is hysterical.

One morning the twins watched closely as I put cream on my face and asked why I did that. I told them it was to make me look younger. One of them stood back, eyed me from toe to ear and solemnly pronounced: "It's working, you're getting shorter!"

The morning came when my love was sorely tested. I am a professional speaker and work out of my home. Children are very paper-intensive, and love to staple, color, cut and draw for hours: so my office was a paper heaven for them. One early morning, our twins had made a horrible discovery: Auntie Beth's seminar handouts aren't pretty enough! I did not know that I had office elves until I arrived at my seminar later that morning. As I opened the box, I found each handout had been carefully decorated with little duckies, birds, trees and flowers.

I was furious. (I took myself much more seriously then.) My ego and professionalism bent out of shape, I managed a weak joke, remembered my rule about "It's SHOWTIME!!!" and got on with the program. All the way home I fumed. I decided that this was IT! There was no reason for this relationship to continue. There had to be some man out there with less baggage. It was time to cut the losses before these little girls got used to me or worse, fell in love with me. And besides, I'm a professional speaker, for heaven's sake. What the heck am I doing in this situation anyway? I'm no young chicken. All my girlfriends are grandmothers, and I'm going to PTA! This is unacceptable. It will ruin my wonderful career... On and on until I pulled into the driveway.

My car is a turbo-5-speed hot rod that has to calm down before I can turn it off. As I sat in the driveway counting to sixty, I heard, "She's home! Auntie Beth is HOME!!! SHHHHH!" I dropped my head to the steering wheel and with heavy heart, resolved to get this over with quickly.

When I walked into the house, eight little arms reached for me and pulled me to the couch. Then they dashed giggling into the back room. Suddenly I heard the strains of the Hawaiian Style Band playing a hula, and out came my four little girls dressed in muumuu. They danced to the song "Love and Honesty" for me and me alone. When it was over, all four piled on top of me, wrapped their arms around my neck and shouted, "We LOVE you, Auntie Beth!!!" And the smallest twin came up close to my ear and whispered in her husky five-year old voice, "Thank you for letting us live with you."

One year later, when the legal wrangling was over, the girls asked their Daddy when he was going to marry me. He told them they had to ask me if that would be OK. When I got home from work, they eagerly pulled me into my room to choose my dress. They said we were all going out to dinner. I asked why and they giggled and said it was a surprise.

We went to Roy's Restaurant in Hawaii Kai. This is an exceptional restaurant, and difficult for little girls intent on popping the question. For them, dinner took a year. They kept jumping up and whispering into Andrew's ear, "NOW Daddy?" And he would say, "No, honey. Soon, soon." Finally, dinner was over and we went outside. In the back of the restaurant, the girls found a garden and pressed me down onto a bench. They pulled single roses from under their muumuu and shoved the tangled, bent buds into my hand. Then they all held hands and shouted, "One-Two-Three. Auntie Beth, will you marry us?" Through tears, I whimpered a quiet, "Yes". Then Andrew got down on one knee and taking my hand in his, asked me to marry him, too. We were married three months later in a rainforest outside of Kailua, Hawaii.

It is not easy, this Love. It is not always safe. And when it is complicated with relatives and ex's and children, it can be frustrating, frightening and damned inconvenient. But when Love is unconditional, it is always the right thing to do.

Beth Terry

"...it is said that
what the caterpillar calls
the end of the world
the master calls
the butterfly..."

Author unknown

"It is not the strongest of the species
that survive, nor the most intelligent,
but the one most responsive to change."

Charles Darwin (1809-1882)

"This is the true joy in life:
Being used for a purpose recognized by yourself
as a mighty one!"

George Bernard Shaw (1865-1950)

Love
&
Relationships

Duke and Retta

A smile from a glamorous cowgirl. Globes burning brightly on the entrance gates to the flowered driveway. Emerald and beige rolling hills as far as the eyes can see, dotted with brown and black cows. Yelping cowboys on horseback moving between the dots, their spurs glinting in the late afternoon sun. Sounds of meadowlarks. Smells of alfalfa, pigs, chickens and horses wafting through dry air.

I slept on a cowhide rug at the foot of their bed. I was five. My parents went east for school. My seven brothers and sisters and I were "farmed out" to parishioners of my Dad's church for a part of the summer. And what a magical summer it was on a working ranch in the Badlands of South Dakota.

I found out that year that I was a scalawag. Duke Ferguson told me so. He was as old as dirt. (Probably over 40!) I had decided that smoking was bad for him, and spent the summer trying to get him to quit. Not only did I lecture him, pointing my stubby five-year old fingers at him, I stole his cigarettes and hid them from him.

Retta, the glamorous cowgirl of shoulder length locks and glittery laugh, thought my antics were hilarious. Duke did not. First I simply threw away his carton of "smokes". He retrieved them easily. He was the one who took out the trash. I tried hiding his smokes under the couch. My brothers slept on the foldaway couch, so when it was pulled out, so were the smokes.

I hid them in plain sight, in the table by the couch. It was the first place he looked. This game went on for weeks. One day. I hit on an idea. Duke never cooked. I hid them in the freezer. And there they stayed for a day, until they were good and frozen. At five years old, the concept of going to the store and simply buying more never occurred to me. (Which was what Duke was doing all along!) And my freezer plan backfired. When Retta retrieved them finally, Duke discovered he liked the taste better, and began freezing all his smokes.

Duke decided I needed a diversion. He took me out and sat me on a horse. My tiny legs shot straight out on either side of this behemoth. It whinnied softly and I fell in love. There was a new kind of peace lying across this warm, live, snorting, breathing mountain. And when Duke began to walk the horse around the yard, I was floating on a furry cloud. I buried my face into it's mane and took in the wondrous horse perfume.

Every day that summer I rode the horses. Never alone: my sister had been kicked by one, and I had enough sense to respect the giants. I loved to watch them being washed. And the sight of the cowboys flying atop their steeds as they herded the cattle embedded itself in my dreams.

In child years, the six weeks at the Ferguson Ranch seemed to last a year. When my dad's dusty station wagon pulled into the ranch, I had to search in memory for life beyond this magical place. I hugged Retta, then Duke swept me into his arms and gave me a bear hug. I slipped my hands into his shirt pocket, lifted his smokes for the last time and, giggling, tossed them to his smiling cowgirl.

Beth Terry

Remember, when you influence a child's life, the memory lasts forever...

Juggling

I look over notes from my earlier courses and realize with my new perspective just how shallow some of my recommendations were. Just as I could not teach time management when I had all the time in the world, I could not teach "going for it" when I had no obstacles other than my own resistance at moving forward.

Suddenly, with four young girls in my life... with a loving man who wants more time from me than I am sometimes physically, mentally and emotionally able to give... with the march of time creating a greater sense of urgency in my days..., I find myself wrestling with these drives inside me. Do I really want those goals I set for myself when I was only with myself? Is my mission a hollow exercise if it is for "the world" but has no room for a real-life-wide-awake-right-there-in-my-face family? Will my workshop words ring true if there is no sisterhood with my audience's pain? Do I have the right to preach "Live up to your potential..." if I cannot find a way through this thicket?

I scream silently at God and ask why this family has come in my fourth decade. I have worked very hard to design a neat package of Beth. I have carefully constructed habits and skills to use what I feel are my best talents. I have organized my life around my strengths and deftly avoided the bright sunlight that might glare down and bare my faults to the world.

I have had total control of my life until now. Until the love came. Now I have to start dealing with buried feelings, buried hurts, buried notions about motherhood and marriage. I juggle my career and my notions of responsibility to "The Relationship" ... or rather, "The RelationshipS." I hear my mother's voice as I tell them, "You will thank me for this when you are older." My businesswoman rears its head and tells me I must be competent. I buy every parenting book and magazine I can find. I read furiously and study the "right" ways to do things... in hopes that doing it right will bring me the same sense of satisfaction I find on stage.

And it doesn't. "Doing parenting right" is not where the satisfaction lies. The small arm around the neck, the innocent love, the sweet voice saying prayers, the neckless-shoulderless awkward drawing of me presented on my birthday, the love "poam" [sic] from a shy eleven-year old, the story about "God and the angle" [sic] — these are the rewards.

And there is a price. There is always a price. I have always prized my clarity. It came with the territory of being alone so much with myself. I was comfortable in that alone-ness, able to meditate for hours at will, able to float through days with no responsibility other than to myself. Clarity does not come so easily now. The mind is full of home lunches, cut knees, tattle-taling and time-outs. There has to be time for on-your-knees

BETHS POAM

Beautiful
Excellent
Terrific
Honest

Thoughtful
Elegant
Reliable
Ravishing
Young

BY CHENTY

Chenty Bonifacio, age 11

118

listening to the little ones. Time for hugs and reassurances. Time for looking over freshly-fingerpainted bears... or is that a pig? And the excited happy chatter distracts the more "serious" thought processes about Managing Employees Efficiently. There *is* a price.

Then I recall that the alone-ness had its price, too. No one to share my successes. Days/weeks without hugs. The danger of believing my own press releases if there were no clear eyed five-year olds saying, "Your hair looks junk today," or "Why do you have to teach grown-ups? Didn't they learn nothin' in school?" And there are few stories in alone-ness, few examples and places of connection with my audience. Few reality checks for me in my material. I wonder at my credibility all those years. How did a busy mother/career woman/softball coach sit patiently through my complicated program on time management? Now my offerings are simpler, easier to use and to remember. More practical. More sublime.

And how did I find the energy day after day to motivate others without love in my life? Unconditional love fuels the soul and expands the being. In our search for partnership, we wrestle with the meaning of togetherness. We tug at each other's time and priorities. We gingerly step around each other's past hurts and do our awkward best to heal. With each passing day, with each conversation, we come closer to the safe place of surrender. Surrender to love, to the inevitable, to joy. We are strong, independent and intense people: eagles trying hard to soar in formation. And we have four eaglets gamely flapping their little wings around us.

This is the best thing and the hardest thing I have ever done. When I am through resisting it all, I imagine I will have found that the contributions to my seminars, to my mission, to my life will be immeasurable. Till then, I accept the fact that I must still learn how to juggle.

Beth Terry

Alisha Bonifacio

"The only gift is a portion of thyself."

Ralph Waldo Emerson (1803-1882)

"It is important to know
what the dearest things in life really are:
the buoyancy of friendship, the support of love."

Burl Burlingame
Honolulu Star Bulletin, 1984

"I like you to the extent that I am comfortable
with myself in your presence."

Olaf Isaachsen, 1987

"The difference between a happy and an
unhappy person is whether or not
their expectations are met."

Beth Terry

"Be good to people.
You don't know
who they are.
You don't know
who they know.
and
You don't know who they might become!"

Beth Terry

House Rules

We love you and we want you to have a happy life.
  If you learn these rules, you will be happy and we
  will all get along better!

- If you turned it on —turn it off.
- If you opened it —close it.
- If you break it —admit it and fix it if you can.
- Do not take what is not yours.
- If it's not yours, and you want to use it,
  ask to borrow it.
- If you borrow it —take good care of it and
  give it back when you said you would.
- If it's not your closet, drawer, cabinet, or purse
  —leave it alone.
- Respect each other —be kind, don't hit or push.
- If you hurt someone, even if it was an
  accident, say you're sorry.
- Always say, "Please," "Thank you," "I'm sorry,"
  "May I," "Excuse me".

- Share.
- Do your chores and help around the house.
- Don't talk with your mouth full.
- Homework before TV.
- Speak only love.
- Do not tattletale on each other.
- No carrying stories from one house to the other.
- Respect the privacy of others.
- Love each other.
- Forgive each other.
- Be grateful for what you have and don't take it for granted.

Beth Terry

"Never do anything in the first year of marriage
that you aren't willing to do
for the rest of your life."

Mom Terry (Elma)
on the occasion of my divorce

"Jealousy is not a measure of love's depth.
It merely records the degree
of the lover's insecurity."

Margaret Mead (1901-1978)

divorce

The divorce was not easy. None of them are. But one day I woke and decided that I wasn't going to participate in the insanity that has become a cultural tradition in America: I wasn't going to be a "victim" of divorce.

I read several books, including *Ano Ano, The Seed* by Kristen Zambucka. She reminded me of something I already knew: there are times when it is right and proper to leave your current situation and move on. My father used to tell me, "Beth, sometimes God lets you go along and go along down the wrong path, waiting for you to see it and change direction. If you don't, He hits you over the head with a frying pan and yanks you out of there."

I realized that I had been hit with a frying pan. I knew in my heart, and had known for some time, that my soon to be ex-husband needed a different kind of partner, and that I did too. I called him and asked for a meeting.

I told him I didn't want to make lawyers rich and thought we could do this in a humane and loving way. He agreed. We made arrangements for the splitting up of property, and decided to take it one more step. We would let our friends know that *they* didn't need to be split up. We would let them know that we were still friends, that we supported each other and that it was OK to love us both.

We then set about repairing the friendship we had prior to our marriage. I asked him how I could be a better wife next time. It wasn't easy to hear (and I wished I had heard it years before), but it was true. I needed to allow my partner to have his say without my loud pronouncements of it being right or wrong. In other words, I needed to become a "safe place" for my husband to vent, and in the process, help us both get in touch with ourselves. I cringed when I thought of the times I had not done that.

He then gave me a chance to tell him some things that could help him be a better husband. (Both our current spouses are very grateful we had that talk!)

We tore up our wedding vows and made divorce vows. We would support each other. We wouldn't belittle each other to old friends. We would honor and treasure the years we had shared together. And, we would not allow the divorce to become rancorous.

There is a tremendous opportunity for growth in crisis. Letting go of old loves, old habits, old beliefs is so hard. It's hard because we don't know that on the other side of this chasm is a far greater peace. When you have not been a good steward of a relationship and allow it to falter beyond repair, you can learn valuable lessons that will buoy you up in the next relationship... if you choose.

I did not choose to be divorced. And I do not recommend it if there is hope for repair. But if it must be, go gently. This is one you once loved. This is one who can find love again if he or she is not damaged by the experience with you. We all walk in each other's hearts. When we have been allowed in, it is important to guard that sacred trust. Who we are is shaped by how we treat the people in our lives.

Beth Terry

To our Friends and Family
from Beth & Stan

In 1984 we each married our best friend. Today, we have chosen to redefine that relationship, and we need your help.

We love and respect each other. And it is time to move on. Shortly we will be divorced, and we choose to accomplish this in a gentle and caring manner. Please keep this in mind as you support us.

We didn't ask you to choose sides at our wedding, so you don't have to choose sides at our divorce.

We also absolve you from expressing anything other than love. We do not need opinions on the viability of the marriage.

We do not need "well-intentioned advice" designed to caution us against the possible evil intentions of the other. We do not want to hear about your third cousin's uncle's best friend who tried to have a gentle divorce and it failed. And we do not want to hear gossip, stories, or anything bad about our soon-to-be-ex-spouse.

In short, we aren't mad at each other. We don't need advice, information or validation of our choice. We need support. Here is what support looks like:

Love us for our courage to make this change.

Invite us to play even when there is only one of us.

When we choose other partners, please give them a chance and don't compare them to our ex-spouse.

If we get crazy and start talking "stink" about the other, gently remind us of our intention and mission to keep this friendly and fair.

Believe with us that this is possible, that it doesn't have to get nasty, and that we still do love each other.

Thank you most of all for the support and love you have shown us these past 10 years of our life together.

We love you and cherish your friendship.

Beth Terry

Forgiveness

On Forgiveness

There will come a day, if it has not yet arrived, when you will make a horrible discovery. All parents do. You will discover that a careless word you tossed off to your son when he was twelve has been deeply imbedded in his memory and continues to injure him twenty years later. You will find that you embarrassed and demoralized your sixteen year old daughter in front of all her friends, and that pivotal moment has been the basis for her child-rearing philosophy this past decade. You will discover that you were a "mean" parent because you did not let your daughter attend an overnight party (because boys would be there). Your son will remember a glare on his first day of kindergarten.

When you are informed of these dreadful mistakes, you will protest that you were young. That your words were careless but not meant to intentionally inflict harm. You will say that you are older now, that you have changed. You will make excuses and struggle mightily to recreate these heinous crimes in your memory. And you will not be able to remember a single moment of those conversations long ago.

In all likelihood, as a parent, you were doing the right thing. If nothing else, you were doing the best you knew how under difficult and stressful circumstances. After all, you were struggling to support a young family. You were still learning about parenting, making it up as you went along. You know all of this now. And your children will not know this until they are old enough to get "the talk" from *their* grown children. After all, life is a dynamic and growing process.

That talk is perhaps the most powerful and special gift you can receive from your children. For it is in that defining moment, as you make your excuses, as you look back and struggle to find a glimmer of a clue in what, for them, was a bonfire event —that you make your own heart stopping discovery... You are now where your parents were when you had "the talk" with them.

Your parents struggled to explain your memories to you when they had none that matched yours. You see, you had one Father, one Mother. They had you and many other children and your experiences were multiplied a hundred times. More than that, they had a life outside their children. A life full of friends, work, co-workers and bosses; mortgages and household worries; health and aging; and just generally trying to make it through their days.

Your parents were doing the best they knew how. Just like you. When you can get that in the deepest part of your soul, forgiveness of your parents' transgressions comes easy...

Let it go. Move on. Love yourself enough to let them be who they are so you can let yourself be who you are.

Beth Terry

On NOT Forgiving

*I recently read an article in "Psychology Today" in which the writer, a Dr. Safer, put forth an argument that it is okay to **not** forgive. I could NOT, not respond:*

According to the American Heritage College Dictionary, the word "forgive" is a derivative of the Old English "ghabh," or more recognizably: "forgi(e)fan." It means to give, to give up, to leave off (anger), to remit. The German counterpart, "fargeban" means to give away.

I have never defined forgiveness the way Dr. Safer does. It is most definitely *not* forgetting and excusing bad behavior. When I forgive, I am not letting the person off the hook; I am removing myself from the power of their action or inaction.

Hawaiian people have a belief that in our relationships, we are connected by cords. When I forgive, I am severing a cord that is controlling me. I am detaching myself from the effect the person has on me. In my world, to not forgive is to continue to allow yourself to be controlled by the offending party. For, as long as you do not forgive, the unforgiven person is still tormenting you.

I have had some heinous things happen to me in my life. The only way I am sane is by detaching myself and cutting the cord. I call that forgiveness. It comes from understanding, from wisdom, from self-knowledge, and from compassion. I do not think "let bygones be bygones" is forgiveness. That attitude is irresponsible and probably suppresses an extreme rage that will surface later.

If you apply the American Heritage definition of forgiveness to Dr. Safer's article, most of her subjects have, in fact, forgiven. They have detached themselves from the damaging parties. They have moved on. They have left off anger and simply recognized that they don't want to be in the offending person's orbit. Perhaps Dr. Safer's subjects can hand this other viewpoint to their well-meaning advice-givers who torment them.

Beth Terry

"I have to forgive them,

...because it is the only way I can be sure they won't be hanging around in my head bothering me."

Forgiveness is *NEVER* about the other person. It *IS* about us. How we react, how we perceive, how we are willing to be jerked around, how we can learn the lesson and be certain not to repeat it to others. How we are willing to live our life instead of cringing under resentment and anger.

God is the one who handles the *Big Job* about redemption. It ain't my job to redeem another by "offering" forgiveness. I forgive because I want to live, I want to love, and I want to have room in my heart for another experience unblocked by the pain of the past.

What could be more destructive than to carry a grudge for forty years? Exactly how long is the holding pattern for anger?

We let the other person win when we expend our energy self-righteously insisting on "holding them to account" or "making sure they know what they *did* to us."

Unforgiving people make me tired.

Beth Terry

Soul Work

Internal Enemy

I have an internal enemy. We all have one. Mine is discouragement.

"Discourage: to take away courage." It demotivates me and takes away hope. It usually strikes when I have put all my energy and enthusiasm, heart and soul into something or someone. And it fails. Or the rewards are not forthcoming.

When I am discouraged, I feel a heavy weight on my chest. Hopelessness. I want to run and hide. I beg God to do something dramatic so I can get 'outta' here. I am looking for the magic "silver bullet."

God chuckles at me and lets it work itself out.

What is my antidote? I write. I analyze. I look for lessons. I do my "gratitudes" — I list ten things for which I am grateful. (A good way to start the day, by the way.)

What is the *real* antidote? Time. In time, I remember who I am. In time, hope reappears. In time, insights are gained. The goal was not mine to have. It may have harmed me. The reward was an intangible I never anticipated. The lesson was necessary for the next stage in my growth... or to kick me out of a complacent rut.

The opposite of discourage is encourage: "to fill with courage." To create hope. To give one the notion that they can move on from this place. Discourage and encourage are yin and yang. The experience of both allows for growth and creates compassion: a way to support and love others on the same path.

I have an internal enemy. What is yours?

Beth Terry

Faith

Faith? You say you don't have faith? Everyday is an act of faith. You take a small piece of paper, write on it, stick it in another folded piece of paper, put a pretty picture in the top right hand corner and go find a blue box on a street corner. When you put your message into that blue box, you actually believe it will go where it is intended.

You have faith when you flip a switch in your house. Faith that a light or a garbage disposal will go on. You have faith when you go into your garage and put your key in the ignition. On the freeway you have faith that no one will be coming towards you on the same side of the freeway; you actually have faith that others will follow the generally accepted rules of the road.

When you get up in the morning, you have faith that you will wake up in the same bed, that the same children will be downstairs, that the sun will come up, the stars will come out and that all the molecules on earth will hold their shape.

You have faith.

And you believe in that which you can't see.

You just forgot.

Beth Terry

Melt Into the Rocks

In spite of myself, I have always known I am blessed. Maybe it's because my mother stuck my name all over the wailing wall in Israel. Maybe it was growing up as a PK (preachers kid). I have felt, as it were, that wherever I go, there are fifteen angels surrounding me.

They whisper in my ear, pull me back from cliffs and generally keep me out of danger. It's a testament to my adventuresome spirit that it takes so many to watch over me. I imagine calmer souls only need a few. When I have done something particularly good-hearted, I can hear them cheer. When I have caused pain, or I am in pain, I feel their tears brush my cheek. It is this special cadre of warriors that tells me I am a daughter of a King who loves me very very much in spite of myself.

It was on the rocks where I learned more about the reality of spiritual life. After a years worth of invitations, I finally accepted a rock-climbing challenge. With much trepidation (I actually took a moment to double check my will before I left the house). I left for the cliffs on the North Shore of Hawai'i. After an arduous hike, there I stood, facing 100 foot cliffs. I was expected to scale these. The people I was with were much hardier men and women who thought this was a piece of cake.

I gamely jumped into the harness and donned the shoes. With great irony I noted that other, lighter climbers only required one person on the other end of the rope. I noticed there was a "back-up" next to my person —not a cheery sign.

There it was: *the Cliff.* There I was: in too deep to quit now. I sighed. I noticed that no one had died yet today and no one seemed particularly concerned. I dug in my fingers the way they showed me. Dug in my toes in crevices waaaaay to small for my suddenly huge feet. Knees aching, I climbed one fearful inch after another, sure that my very breath depended on this knuckle and that big toe grasping rock for all they were worth.

And then, the rock wall was leaving me. My fingers and toes gave out and I was falling. Only, ...not really. I was bouncing, like a babe in an infant swing. Boing, boing, boing. I began to giggle. I didn't die. I had a person on the ground holding a top rope for me. I looked up at the rope curling through the metal ring at the cliff top, and then down at my balancer on the ground. She grinned and told me "she had me" and I was safe.

I got it. When you fall off the rocky cliffs of life, look closely at the ground. God is smiling up at you and saying, "Go on, I have you. You're safe." Your fears will melt into the rocks.

Beth Terry

New Year's Eve Meditation
December 31, 1994

Right now there are four children laughing and playing outside my house. They are on new bicycles and skates and loving every moment. I sit here wondering about my life. Perhaps I should borrow from them: they don't wonder about their lives, they wonder how butterflies can sit on a leaf, why skin starts to get wrinkly, why God gave us arms, and if Auntie Beth's skin is white because the face cream she uses every night is white.

Aunty Beth

I wonder about my life. How did I wind up here? Is this the path God intended for me? What am I to do? Should I take on this awesome responsibility and become their stepmother? How do I make peace with their mother? How do I live in this culture that is so different from mine? How do I juggle seminars and children and a man... and not in that order?

Liandra Bonifacio

Last year I wrote that I will love Beth more. Have I? Did I follow my heart? Did I keep in touch with my higher spirit? I said I would read more. Little did I know that it would mean reading *The Hippopotamus Ate The Teacher* and other great literary works. I vowed to play more. I have played: tea party, clapping games, pretend school and card tricks. I said I would focus on helping healthy people get healthier —I didn't know they would be five, seven and ten years old. I said I wanted to train more —I have trained how to measure water, how to tell time, how to tie a shoe, how to break bread up for turkey dressing and how to make cranberry sauce for Thanksgiving.

I wanted to learn more. And *have* I learned: how to be patient; how to give a time-out and still be loving; how to convince five year old twins to go to bed, and how to wake them up in the morning without having them cry. I have learned to say, "Does this **look** like a playground?" when they get rowdy. I have learned to stop what I am doing and *really* listen. I have learned to get down on my knees so we can look each other in the eyes. I have learned how to draw a pig, how to make an angel, how to love.

In my December 1993 resolutions, I said I wanted companionship: someone to help me play more, to be a part of a family, to have kids around to love and be loved unconditionally. It is all here. In one short year my prayers were answered.

And, "they" (the all-powerful they) always say "Be careful what you ask for... you might get it!" Be careful because all requests have a cost. I have lost freedom and free time. I have been frustrated with family issues. My exercise and meditation time has been sharply curtailed.

But my new roommates, the short members of this household and my husband, have a way of making it better. They are adept at coming in at the right time to hug me, love me, or draw me a love note, and I am OK.

What am I about? What am I supposed to be doing?? I don't know. Perhaps this is a year for waiting.

They have come into the house. Andrew and the kids are in the next room. He is helping the twins with their homework. What an amazing, incredible man. He is so calm and strong. He commands their respect and love and they obey him. He puts up with no nonsense, but he does it in such a way that they don't seem to mind his strictness; indeed, I believe they revel in it. What a precious gift he is for them. So few girls have fathers who get involved, who take care of the day to day stuff, who teach them discipline and consideration. They won't ever really know how different he is. But someday they will realize how precious he is.

Last night we were watching a TV show where the father died. I was quietly crying and realized the kids were watching me. One of the five year olds climbed up on my lap to comfort me. She asked me how long it had been since my daddy got hurt, then hugged me and patted me on the shoulder, "It's OK, Auntie, it's OK." I hope they won't have to know this pain for a long, long time. I was 36. That is too young to lose your father. There are no words to soothe the loss of a parent. And when a father is as awesome as theirs, the pain will be that much greater.

Again I am reminded to live in the present and not think about those things. The future will come soon enough. It all becomes a memory so fast. The childhood years will be memories in no time, and Andrew and I will sit around wondering how in God's name we did it. How did we keep this relationship alive in the middle of all these children? How did we juggle so many lives? How? Just like everyone else — you do what you do one breath at a time. And one day you look back and wonder.

So, 1995, here I come. Complete with children and a man who loves me unconditionally. I come into the new year with a great deal of what I asked for not 365 days ago. So grant me again my wishes. Grant me the courage, abundance and opportunities to do whatever is called for me to do next year.

Thank you, Divine Creator for all the gifts you have given me. Bless me with the courage, wisdom and foresight to use them in the best way possible. And thank you for another year. *AMEN*

Beth Terry

"Never do anything
that impoverishes your soul..."

Beth Terry

"With God, you never fly solo..."

Beth Terry

The Gardener

We worked in the yard yesterday from 6:30 in the morning to 8:00 pm, clearing overgrowth and trimming back trees to let in more light.

As is often the case, that night, my day's activities wound themselves into my dreams.

For weeks I had been harboring a resentment. Not towards anyone specifically, just an irritation that was growing unattended.

In my dream, a large, gentle hand reached in and pulled out that weed, saying, "Well, we don't need that here anymore."

Instantly, I felt a relief. I had gotten so used to the darkness that I hadn't noticed it till the light came back.

Perhaps it is just that easy. Give your doubts, fears and pain over to The Gardener and let the weeds be pulled up — roots and all.

You don't need them anymore...

Beth Terry

Miracles

The Miracle of Christmas

The Christmas after I lost my father, I couldn't even think of a tree. I bought one and never took it out of the bucket in the garage. Instead I hung a few decorations from the chandelier in the dining room and half-heartedly went through the motions. Since Dad was a minister, and Christmas is the "heavy season" for all that religious stuff, I could barely sit through the services.

Then, the miracle. I was sitting in church for the midnight service feeling very lost and sad. The church was packed and people were lining up on the aisle stairs (the church was a theater in the round with pews going down the stairs and the pulpit in the center at the bottom of the horseshoe). I was in the first row. In the darkened church, candles reflected in floor to ceiling windows... an entire congregation of angels joining us in the eerie darkness.

While we sang "Away in a Manger", I heard a rustle near my feet. A young mother had brought her newborn to church and laid her on a blanket on the floor. There before me was the miracle of Christmas. It was as if my dad had sent a message of redemption. That this is, after all, why we celebrate... not the madness of the mall, not the tree, not the family gatherings. Just a simple child. A message from God that the world must go on. That even in the face of death there is this life to be lived, this soul to express, this promise to be kept.

In that moment, peace washed over me.

And whenever I felt sad or missed my dad, I closed my eyes and saw that little child. And, years later, when I was reeling from my divorce, I saw that young mother and her then-five-year old daughter. Again the reminder, again an affirmation of life, and once again I was blessed.

Look for the miracles around you. They are messages of love. Those who have gone before us are all around us. Dad was such a light spirit, that I know he is laughing with the angels now. Remember that.

Beth Terry

Angels

Angels are not always ethereal beings:
winging ghost-shadows in the mind. After many
a tearful night, when God had to listen to sobs of
"Why?, Where?, How? and When?," my answers
came from a stranger in passing. A word, a question, a gesture, a TV program or a newspaper article
—and my "angel" responded for God.

And I knew.... I knew.

Beth Terry

"People have asked me why I chose to be a dancer.
I did not choose, I was chosen to be a dancer,
and with that, you live all your life."

Martha Graham (1894-1991)

"Evil only wins
when a good heart
begins to hate."

Beth Terry

"Integrity prevails."

Buckminster Fuller (1895-1983)

"Wise is the one
who gives up
what he cannot have
in order to keep
what he cannot lose."

Author unknown

"There are only two lasting bequests
we can leave our children:
roots and wings."

Author unknown

"The world needs healthy people.
There are too many damaged souls out there
and we need you to
**stop living down to your excuses and
start living up to your potential!!!**"

Beth Terry

Transformation

Legacy

My father left when we least expected it. He had been the life of the party the night before when he and Mom went to entertain clients of the outplacement company where he worked. He had been a Presbyterian Minister for 25 years, and one day decided he could reach a lot more souls helping people find jobs after layoffs and by going on the National Speaker Circuit.

I'm a lot like my Dad. Actually, watching him in the pulpit all those years convinced me that this was a great way to live: you stand up and say a lot of good stuff, then, if people are moved by it, they give you money. So, I majored in speech and psychology with a smattering of business thrown in. But I never really committed to what Dad did... until he left.

He didn't know he was leaving. He had just gotten his body working pretty good: survived some prostate surgery; got his weight down; knocked cholesterol on its butt, and jogged regularly.

It was after one of those jogging sessions that he left. Well, it took a few days longer, but a good portion of him left that morning. He came home from an early run to get ready for work. He saw the hot tub was percolating and thought my Mom had turned on the Jacuzzi for him. When he stuck a toe in, he learned too late that there had been a malfunction of the thermostat. He lost his balance and fell into the 212° water.

His primal brain took over when the heat hit him. It propelled him out of the boiling water, across the pavement into the pool. He yelled for Mom to wake up and get an ambulance. His trip to Sherman Oaks Burn Center was excruciating. He had lost 94% of his skin.

My mother was in shock. She called her eight children and told us to pray for Daddy, because "He did a dumb thing; he got burned in the hot tub." Because she was so numb, we didn't realize at first how serious it was. I mentioned to some friends to pray for Dad because he was in Sherman Oaks Burn

Center. When they heard where he was they said, "It has nineteen beds and it is the *only* burn center west of the Mississippi. This is serious. Go home NOW." I called the hospital and talked to him for a few minutes, telling him I'd try to get there soon. He told me not to worry; he'd be fine.

When I arrived in Los Angeles, I found out that I was the only person allowed to talk with him before they put the tubes down his throat. The nurse was so impressed with a call from way out here in exotic Hawai'i that she ignored hospital rules and put him on the phone.

Within three days my seven brothers and sisters arrived and set up camp in the burn hospital. We were draped over tables and chairs in the waiting rooms and cafeteria twenty-four hours a day. When Dad's morphine dropped his blood pressure dangerously low, the nurses would wake us and we would crowd around his bed, hold hands and sing the old camp songs, "How Great Thou Art," "The Old Rugged Cross," "Blessed Be the Tie That Binds." Dad's blood pressure would soar and we would file back to our restless tabletop sleep.

At different times, we would sneak in for a visit alone with him. He could not talk because of the tubes. I thought this was a cruel cosmic joke. Dad was known for waxing eloquent and sermonizing every time we saw him. Here was his last chance, and he couldn't say a word.

Tuesday morning, I went into the room to be with him. Mom was just leaving and said he had lapsed into a coma at dawn. I placed my hands on his heavily bandaged arms and prayed, leaning over his comatose form. Suddenly, I felt a surge of power and was thrown from his body. I fell back into the chair, unable to move and began to sob.

With surreal energy, I pulled myself up again and prayed over him. Again, I was thrown from the body. My brother ran into the room. He had seen a blue light and thought I had been electrocuted by one of the machines. I stood there, dazed and watched. Soon, Dad fluttered his eyes and woke up.

That afternoon, the doctors said that Dad had deep fourth degree burns from his waist down and that more than three fourths of his body was no longer functioning. He said they would have to do some incredibly painful scraping on the burns to keep him even marginally alive, and he might not survive the pain. He was at the maximum amount of pain-killer a human could take. We had to make a decision whether to approve the scraping or to pull life support.

The agony, fear and hopelessness surrounding such a conversation is one no black-and-white legislation can encompass. It is incomprehensible that anyone outside our situation could ever pretend to make that wrenching decision for our family.

We were told that there was a formula for survival in burn cases. They take the percentage of the body that is burned and add it to the age of the person. The total is the patient's chance of *not* making it. My Dad was 62 and was burned over 94% of his body. We could keep the upper half of his body in excruciating pain, or we could let him go home.

He made the decision for us. When we went to the room to pray over him, he looked up and began gesturing his mummy-wrapped arm toward the left-hand corner of the ceiling. He bowed his head, making eye contact with the angels. When we asked if he wanted to go, he nodded as vigorously as we had seen him since the accident. We decided that if he were supposed to make it, he would make it no matter what we did. We sobbed as support was turned off. Within twenty minutes, the soul of an incredible human being left the planet to join his angels.

My former husband, Stan, flew up for the funeral. He has a beautiful baritone voice, and Mom wanted him to honor Dad with "How Great Thou Art." In the packed church, his deep voice rang out into the rafters. At the verse beginning "When I shall die…" he broke down and my sister Carol began singing to support him. Then my whole family chimed in, then the choir and then the entire church. The magic of nearly one thousand voices rising in chorus carried Dad's soul to the heavens.

On the plane home to Hawai'i, we sat next to an old Hawaiian Kapuna (spiritual teacher). I told her of my bolt of lightening experience over my Dad's bed. She patted me on the knee and said, "No worry. Was good. Was Daddy sending you his mana. His power to do his work. You are blessed my little keiki. You will do well."

Two years later, I had a dream. My father was standing at the foot of my bed. He said, "Beth, when you die, what will you have stood for? When you die, what will you be remembered for? When you die, will your soul celebrate your life?"

On the second anniversary of his accident, I started my career as a professional speaker. He stands on stage with me at every session.

Beth Terry

Coming Home to Myself

As a professional speaker, I have learned that to walk in other people's minds is a sacred trust. I have learned to hold this trust in my heart and ask always for God's grace and wisdom as I share my story. I have learned that we all have a light shining deep within; that we are all lonely; and that we truly do need each other. I am learning how to trust, and I am learning how to find the way home to myself.

Beth Terry

dead

We stood at the foot of the bed.
Wrapped like a mummy he reached for the ceiling.
Holding hands to stave off, what?
We bravely watched.
The breath left him.
My bible-beating sister swore for the first time.
He was there. He was not there. That's it.

dead is
permanent.
unchangeable.
Immutable...
over.

Life is dynamic.
Everything in life changes.
If you don't like your life,
hang around.
It will change.

Dead mystifies and frightens us.
We invent names for dead:

deceased, passed on, passed over, transmuted,
kicked the bucket, bought the farm, expired,
went to that big (fill in the blank) in the sky,
went to be with Jesus, Buddha, Karma, ...
It is none of those...
dead is dead.

Gone
forever.
No recourse.
No coming back for a retry.
No "Oops, I was just kidding,
I want to be alive again."

The heart stops.
The breath stops.
One minute there.
Now, gone.

Is our body a "space suit"?
A malleable carrying case for the soul?
When my space suit dies,
my body is dead.

My father is dead.
He lost the cover to his carrying case.
His skin was burned off and the rest of him let go.
I had to let go.

How can you lose your skin?
I looked at my skin with wonder for a long time after.
I didn't care about wrinkles anymore...
Skin –having it– was more important.

He's dead.
Gone.
No phone calls.
No way to check up on how he's doing.
They don't have an answering machine in heaven.

It's permanent.
Dead.

I miss him.

I wrote this in the lobby of the burn hospital an hour after Dad died.
                                                              Beth Terry

Voice of an Angel

Israel Kamakawiwo'ole died today. His name resonates like his songs. Today, Hawaii's airwaves are full of his sweet voice. As I drive down the Waianae coast towards Honolulu, a DJ on Hawaiian 105.1 calls out to all the listeners who love "Iz" to turn on their headlights, in memory of the man who touched our souls.

Tears well up as I listen to the love song recorded a few months ago for his wife: "Let the world stop turning, let the sun stop burning, let them tell me life's not worth going through. When it all falls apart, I will know deep in my heart, the only dream that matters has come true, In this life, I was loved by you..." *

Suddenly, I glance in my rearview mirror. Every car in the four lanes behind me has flashed on their lights. Chicken skin paints my arms and tears wash my face. God is truly in these moments. Isolated in our metal cars, we still reach out and connect.

The resiliency of the human spirit;
the need to connect is ultimately
what will save us from ourselves.
In this life, Love.

Beth Terry

*Song recorded by Israel Kamakawiwo'ole, "In Dis Life"
Mountain Apple Records, Honolulu, Hawaii (800) 882.7088
Lyrics by Mike Reid and Allen Shamlin,
Almo Music Corporation, Los Angeles, California.
Used by permission

Obituary

A morning will come and we will turn to page B2 of the morning paper. And in crisp bold lettering will be your name. Along side will be your age, date of death and next of kin. What will be written in the column? What contribution? Who loved you?

John Mitchell, the famed Republican Attorney General in the seventies is best known for his part in Watergate and for his ever-dramatic wife Martha. He died in 1988.

Throughout his life he championed many causes. Lived, loved, fathered children, gave to charities and generally tried to live a good life.

He was embroiled in one of this century's best-known scandals, Watergate, and his obituary headlines read: "Watergate Player John Mitchell Dead at 64."

Some of us will not even merit an obituary longer than a few inches. Some of us will have no one but family show up at the funeral. Others will be like Shannon Smith, University of Hawaii football player who drowned saving the life of his coach's young son.

It is fragile, this life. Each precious day gives us choices: choices about holding on or letting go; about feeding our soul or destroying it; about greed, jealousy, bitterness, and rage; or, choosing love, detachment, freedom and joy.

Each of us has been given so many days on the planet and only the Master knows the number. What do you do with those days? How do you choose?

Beth Terry

Death of A Policeman

Her husband died today. She sits in disbelief, numbly working through the words she will say to their four year old son. Her hands glide over the arm of the couch where last night her husband sat and caressed her hair. Silently she takes back every angry word ever spoken. She fights to remember just what their last words were. You are supposed to remember your last words. She strains to hear his voice, but only remembers the radio reporting the shooting and the call from his Captain. Something about gang violence and retribution. She bargains with God— "He was just doing his job!" She looks at the ceiling and prays that this is just the same bad dream every policeman's wife has from time to time.

They come in waves. "He was a hero." "It always happens to the good ones." "So young..." The table groans under mounds of food. She can't eat. He can never eat again, how can she eat? They fumble with awkward silences, foolish advice, "It was probably fast, he probably didn't feel any pain." Pain? Is there anything but pain?

Classmates file in. They were recruits together. Slowly the room fills with memories: "When we were at the academy...", "Do you remember the technical driving drills...", "He stood up for me...", "I always knew I could count on him...", "We said we'd go sailing one day..." Their aching sadness mixed with guilt; they know it could have been any one of them. They shake their heads and drift out. At home, they hug their children, suddenly grateful for life, for family, for wives and husbands, for another chance.

The business side of death intrudes. "Did he leave a will?" "Where shall we bury him?" "The department will take care of details." She walks in a daze to their room and finds the uniform she pressed for him this morning. She checks for the love note in his breast pocket and leaves it there. The officer takes away the last uniform her husband will ever wear.

They all leave and she is alone with her sleeping son. She turns on every light in the house, as if to wait for his return from patrol. She sleeps fitfully, then joins her laughing, young husband in her dreams.

And in houses all across town, moonlight streams down on his fellow officers, sobbing in their sleep as grateful wives and husbands silently say a prayer of thanks for one more day.

Beth Terry

Dedicated to the men and women who have served with my husband on the Honolulu Police Force.

"Don't you ever want to know
how all this will turn out?
The problem is, when you find out,
you're done!"

Beth Terry

Look for the Light

I sat in church at the Midnight Mass gazing at the reflection of the congregation holding candles in the dimmed church. It looked as if the candles were holding the people and I got it! I understood what my father meant when he said,

"All of us have a light inside of us. That's the soul. Instead of seeing something you don't like about a person —look for the light.

Look for the light."

Rev. Condon Terry

Beth Terry

Lights of the World

Beth Terry

if God
blew up the planet
and all the humans on it,

all that would be left
— should any eye survive to see it —
would be the lights
of millions
of souls...

And
the earth
and
sky
would be one
twinkling mass.

Some lights would be
                dim,
                barely perceptible,
                and
        some would vie
                in brilliance
                        with the sun.

                And
                upon
                one
        loud,
thundering shout,
        God
                would call
                        Her souls home,

        and
        the
                lights
                        would
                                stream
                                        heavenward

        forever

You Get What You Want

An atheist died.

There was nothing, and he said, "Huh, looks like I was right all along."

Suddenly he became aware of a shadowy figure. In a quivering voice he asked, "Who are you?"

"I'm God," the figure replied.

"B-B-But - I thought there was no God or Heaven."

"Well," said God, "there is one immutable and non-negotiable law in the Universe. I love my creations so much that I will give to each of you whatever you want. So, those of you who believe passionately that I am a vengeful and angry God, will have to pay for every mistake you made in your lifetime. If you believe I am a forgiving God, you will get Forgiveness."

"But what about me?" The atheist asked.

"You, my friend, will get oblivion. I just wanted you to see what your option was."

Beth Terry

Put all sadness from thee,
for it is the sister of doubt and anger.
It is the most mischievous of all spirits and
the worst to the servants of God.
Learn now, O unwise man!
how it troubleth the Holy Spirit;
remove therefore, sadness from thyself and
afflict not the Holy Spirit
which dwelleth within thee.

The Shepherd of Hermas, circa 142-157 A.D.

Here is a truth about analyzing life...
the harder you try, the more difficult it becomes.
Life is very simple...
take care of each other;
love at least one other person besides yourself;
do something useful;
never give up.

Beth Terry

I found this while huddling in a rainstorm under a tree next to a wall in Sacramento. As I pushed in further to avoid the rain, I looked at the wall and on a brass plaque was this saying.

Remember
that the meaning of life
is to build a life as if it were a
work of art.

Start working on this great work of art
called your own existence.

Remember the importance of
self-discipline, study the great sources
of wisdom, and
remember that
Life is a celebration.

Abraham Joshua Heschel
(1907-1972)

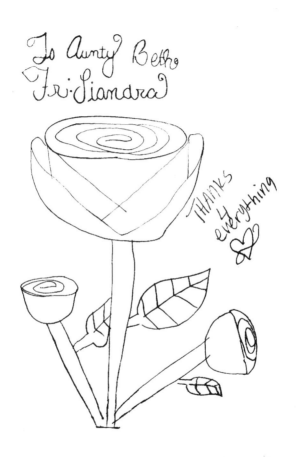

Liandra Bonifacio, age 11

Beth Terry portrait by Joel Karesh
Int'l Convention Photography

About the Author

Beth Terry is President of Pacific Rim Seminars, based in Honolulu, Hawaii. Active in Training and Management since 1976, she has spoken to more than 200,000 people (80,000 of those since 1989). She has presented seminars in Canada, Singapore, Thailand, Malaysia, Indonesia, Guam and across the United States.

Her dynamic motivational presentations include "Stop Living Down to Your Excuses and Start Living UP to Your Potential!", "Getting Out of Overwhelm", "Making Change Work for You!" , "What A Difference You Make!" and "Relationships: Can't We All Just Get Along?"

Beth formerly was Executive Director and Producer of the television show "Making Your Life Work." She is married to a policeman and together they raise his four beautiful school-age daughters.

Seminars/Training

Participants in Beth Terry's seminars have said that the programs are "dynamic," "inspirational," "enlightening," "funny," "practical," and "life-changing." No matter what the topic, Beth strives to awaken the real self inside her listeners. She helps us to laugh at ourselves and see our challenges from a broader perspective.

In her "Managing Stress" and "Getting out of Overwhelm" presentations, she reminds us that we are the authors and directors of our own movies: if you got yourself into it, you can get yourself out of it.

Her "Managing Change" seminar reminds us of the normal fears and declines in productivity which occur when change happens. She helps us move through despair to hope.

In "Stop Living Down to Your Excuses and Start Living UP to Your Potential!!", she drives us past our fears and blocks into greater heights.

And her most popular keynote, "What a Difference You Make!" asks us to capture the essence of who we truly are and share that gift.

All these programs can be tailored to your audience, and all can be presented in breakout session format or in keynote. For more information, check Beth's website:

http://www.BethTerry.com

or call

808.672.5008

Order Form:

Telephone orders: **808.672.5008**
Fax orders: **808.672.5287**
Online orders: **orders@BethTerry.com**
US Mail orders

Ms. Beth Terry
PO Box 29600
Honolulu, HI 96820-2000 SA

Please send _____ copies of *Walking in a Crowd of Angels*

$15 @ $20/ea (tax included) $ _____

S/H: $4. ($2 each add'l copy) $ _____

Total $ _____

Name _____

Address _____

_____

City _____ State _____ Zip _____ - _____

Telephone _____ Fax _____

email _____

Payment:
☐ Check or money order (Make payable to: Pacific Rim Seminars)
☐ Visa   ☐ Mastercard   ☐ AMEX   ☐ Discover

Card number _____

Name on card _____ Exp. date ____ / __

Signature _____

visit our website
www.BethTerry.com

Order Form:

Telephone orders: **808.672.5008**
Fax orders: **808.672.5287**
Online orders: **orders@BethTerry.com**
US Mail orders:

> Ms. Beth Terry
> PO Box 29600
> Honolulu, HI 96820-2000 ;A

Please send _____ copies of *Walking in a Crowd of Angels*

~~$15~~ @ $20/ea (tax included) $ _____

S/H: $4. ($2 each add'l copy) $ _____

Total $ _____

Name _____

Address _____

_____

City _____ State _____ Zip _____ - _____

Telephone _____ Fax _____

email _____

Payment:
☐ Check or money order (Make payable to: Pacific Rim Seminars)
☐ Visa   ☐ Mastercard   ☐ AMEX   ☐ Discover

Card number _____

Name on card _____ Exp. date ____ / ___

Signature _____

visit our website
www.BethTerry.com